Lent Study Guide

Encounters with Jesus

Joel Edwards

CWR

Published 2009 by CWR, Waverley Abbey House, Waverley Lane, Farnham, Surrey GU9 8EP, UK.
Registered Charity No. 294387. Registered Limited Company No. 1990308.

See back of book for list of National Distributors.

Concept development, editing, design and production by CWR

Cover image: iStockphoto

Printed in Croatia by Zrinski

ISBN: 978-1-85345-535-3

Contents

Introduction

It's not that people don't feel guilty any more. Most of us still get a pang of guilt if we tell a big lie, sleep around or even kick the cat in a fit of temper. It's just that we live in a culture which has successfully detached the idea of guilt from the reality of God. Which means that 'sin' is an anachronism, and to call someone a 'sinner' is an offensive condemnation rather than hope of redemption. And if sin is outdated, it means no one needs to be saved from anything; which makes Easter just another public holiday; which is a real problem because God still takes it seriously.

So while Christians talk about sin, it turns out that we are increasingly using in-house language which we understand, but which means very little to anyone else.

Telling Christians that 'Sin is sin!' is like saying 'Gin is gin!' It makes perfect sense if someone has already helped you to identify the taste. A century ago talk of sin would have been a very natural thing because everybody knew roughly what everybody else meant by it. At the very least it was a recognisable idea which meant that our behaviour fell outside God's expectations and we had some kind of obligation to think about forgiveness. At worst it invoked ideas of God's retribution for a warped, fallen nature and a condition so depraved that it begged for God's mercy. So when the famous eighteenth-century American evangelist Jonathan Edwards preached about 'sinners in the hands of an angry God', the people of New England responded to the message because they understood it. A colleague who studied American history told me that her class found this story bizarre!

In recent years 'sin' has ceased to be a word which Christians and non-Christians share in the same way. In the twenty-first century it may be as much a 'sin' to miss the lottery roll-over by a single digit as it is to murder a child.

All of this is much more than an academic discussion. It goes to the very heart of our Christian faith and the meaning of Lent. In the absence of a common vernacular about 'sin', we now have an urgent mission: to help people rediscover the awfulness of that condition which separates us from the love of God and which makes the life, death and resurrection of Jesus so central to our faith. It is not to gloss over the impact of sin; neither is it to insist brazenly that if 'sin' was good enough for Paul, it's good enough for me! There is no harm in speaking Mandarin to the Chinese, but it is helpful to work at learning a new language if we are living in Spain.

Our Lent study will put Jesus where He belongs – at the very centre of our thoughts. But we will try to find some other images and current ideas which may act as cultural dictionaries when it comes to talking about the reality of sin and the meaning of Lent.

Each 'Encounter with Jesus' will point us to a biblical text. At the heart of each study is an account of an encounter with Jesus through which we can explore each of the contemporary themes, and which leads us on to some application, group exercises and a final prayer for devotion.

The study uses Psalm 51 as a common thread running sequentially through each of the six studies. It is meant to give some continuity while also providing an Old Testament complement to the New Testament encounters with Jesus.

Each study also has a built-in 'To-Do Moment', which is aimed deliberately at getting us to think and act on what we have learned. No one ever came to Jesus and left the same. I hope this encounter will also make a difference in your life.

Jesus and Bad Stuff

Icebreaker

Either in teams or as individuals, have a competition for the best acronym for LENT. You may want to have the best and the runner-up read out or presented in the wider church service the following Sunday with a small gift!

> I do not understand what I do. For what I want to do I do not do, but what I hate I do. (Romans 7:15)

A Story

When I was the pastor of a small congregation in the East End of London some years ago, the Sunday School superintendent gave me a very tough assignment. She asked me to take the class of 8- to 11-year-olds. That was scary enough, but what really made me think that I was being punished was the fact that the Sunday School lesson that day was on the topic of sin! Imagine having to wrestle with one of the most difficult theological issues with a group of 8- to 11-year-olds.

So I did what any nervous teacher does and began with questions. 'Who can tell me what sin is?' I asked sheepishly. A small tidal wave of hands floated upwards. Cassandra seemed to be bursting at the seams.

'Yes, Cassandra. What do you think it is?'

'Sin is bad stuff!' she said with an air of someone who had just said something very important. And indeed she had, because I have used that illustration on more occasions than I care to remember. I use it for one special reason: it's one of the most graphic and yet accessible descriptions of what Christians call 'sin' that I ever heard. And every time I mention it to Christians and non-Christians alike, it seems to make sense because it describes the tension between right and wrong which all of us know so well.

Encounter with Jesus: Acts 9:1–9

Meanwhile, Saul was still breathing out murderous threats against the Lord's disciples. He went to the high priest and asked him for letters to the synagogues in Damascus, so that if he found any there who belonged to the Way, whether men or women, he might take them as prisoners to Jerusalem. As he neared Damascus on his journey, suddenly a light from heaven flashed around him. He fell to the ground and heard a voice say to him, 'Saul, Saul, why do you persecute me?'

'Who are you, Lord?' Saul asked.

'I am Jesus, whom you are persecuting,' he replied. 'Now get up and go into the city, and you will be told what you must do.'

The men travelling with Saul stood there speechless; they heard the sound but did not see anyone. Saul got up from the ground, but when he opened his eyes he could see nothing. So they led him by the hand into Damascus. For three days he was blind, and did not eat or drink anything.

Very few people in the New Testament exemplify this tension between good and evil as Saul of Tarsus did. A Hebrew scholar and champion for Judaism, Saul was a death sentence on horseback looking for Christians. His zeal made him an executioner and his love for truth made him a persecutor of the Way. For Saul bad stuff meant threats and murder.

His dramatic encounter with Jesus on the road to Damascus was a turning point. The blinding light from heaven had shown up Saul's bad stuff and this overpowering event was not the end of a process: it was to be the start of a long clean-up exercise in his life. It also uncovered something else: Saul's attitudes and destructive behaviour didn't just affect other people.

Jesus also took it personally. Saul's guilt had a lot to do with God. Jesus said, 'You're persecuting me!' Perhaps more than anything else, Saul (who came to be known as Paul) must have been struck by the realisation that he had actually been opposing the very God he thought he had been defending. His encounter with Christ made it clear to him that he was opposing more than a sectarian idea: he was actually standing in God's way.

Paul's encounter with Jesus wasn't just for his benefit, however. It meant a radical reversal which would shape the Early Church and change the world. Paul's encounter with Jesus is a powerful reminder that God always accepts us as He finds us but doesn't leave us as He meets us. He always has something better in mind for us.

Reflections from Psalm 51:1-3

Have *mercy* on me, O God,
according to your *unfailing love*;
according to your great *compassion*
blot out my transgressions.
Wash away all my iniquity
and cleanse me from my sin.
For I know my transgressions,
and my sin is always before me.

This is an opportunity for some group reflection on how the psalm relates to us today. In our passage a number of key words have been highlighted. Take some time to consider how you understand those words. Do they mean the same thing, or are they very different in their meaning for us? And then ask how they relate to the character and work of Jesus.

Application

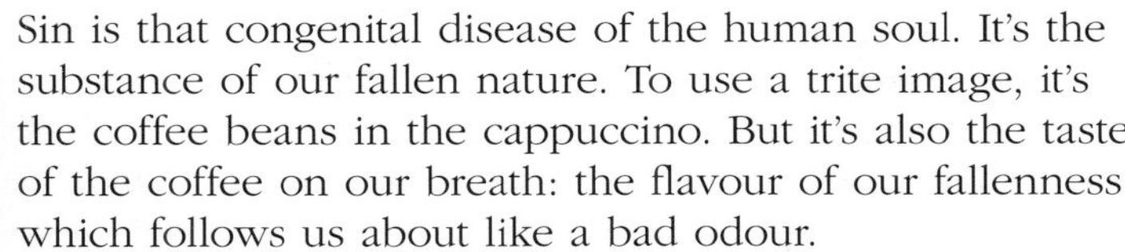

Sin is that congenital disease of the human soul. It's the substance of our fallen nature. To use a trite image, it's the coffee beans in the cappuccino. But it's also the taste of the coffee on our breath: the flavour of our fallenness which follows us about like a bad odour.

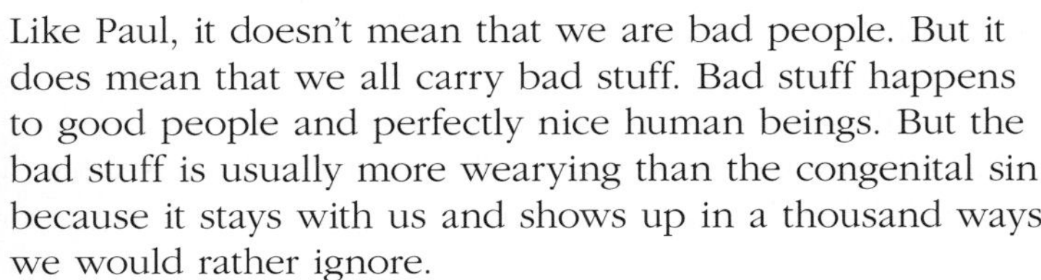

Like Paul, it doesn't mean that we are bad people. But it does mean that we all carry bad stuff. Bad stuff happens to good people and perfectly nice human beings. But the bad stuff is usually more wearying than the congenital sin because it stays with us and shows up in a thousand ways we would rather ignore.

It can be as mundane as a really bad habit which dominates our lives and forces us into reluctant daily repentance. It's the petty pride we keep saying 'sorry' for and that absurd argument which stops us from praying properly. But as Paul would remember for ever, it could also be the heinous act of murder which will remain with us for the rest of our lives.

Everybody has bad stuff, because everybody has the congenital condition. Our bad stuff has multiple manifestations and a wide range of ways in which we explain it away, so that parents describe it in one way, a policeman in another, and a politician in yet another! But it all comes down to the things we would rather not do and say and the things we really should have said and done. It amounts to the things which hurt us and the people we love. Our bad stuff emerges from the radioactive substance of the human soul. Our sinfulness is a part of our nature of sin.

It's in us and all around us. Bad stuff is on every news channel every hour of every week. It stalks in dark alleys and is alive and well in the board room. It's the reason why we gasp in disbelief at acts of atrocity or wilful violence. Our bad stuff ignites our family feuds, tribalism, terror and hostilities.

Bad stuff confuses us because it stands in constant contradiction with what is good and noble in us. At the best of times everything in us wants to do what's right and yet so much within us reaches out for what is less than good. The bad stuff we carry fogs up the good stuff. We are never sure which of the two people see in us most. Thankfully, Jesus saw more than a persecutor in Paul. What He saw was a defender of the faith and that's what He made out of him.

A To-Do Moment!

Each week we want to give the group time to reflect and to make a note of what they feel the Holy Spirit is asking them to do about what has been said so far. This is not to pull us down, but to lift us up for Lent.

Jesus – A Quick Response: Luke 6:45

> 'The good man brings good things out of the good stored up in his heart, and the evil man brings evil things out of the evil stored up in his heart.'

Discussion Starters

1. How would you evaluate Cassandra's view of sin? Is 'bad stuff' too simplistic when dealing with such a serious issue as sin?

2. We talk of sinfulness and a nature of sin. Can we make any such distinction?

3. How would you explain the relationship between the things we experience around us and the things which take place within us?

4. Have you ever experienced a 'Damascus' moment? Can you describe what happened, and how your life changed as a result?

5. Can you imagine how Saul felt after his encounter on the road? What do you think was the significance of his temporary blindness and fasting?

6. Take a moment to think of a time when God may have shown you 'unfailing love'. How might we show God's mercy and compassion to other people?

A Prayer

Grant us, O Lord, the royalty of inward happiness and the serenity that comes from living close to Thee. Daily renew in us the sense of joy, and let Thy eternal spirit dwell in our souls and bodies, filling every corner of our hearts with light and gladness. So that, bearing about with us the infection of a good courage, we may be diffusers of life, and meet all that comes, of good or ill, even death itself, with gallant and high-hearted happiness; giving Thee thanks always for all things.

Robert Louis Stevenson, 1850–94

Jesus and Negative Equity

Retracing Our Steps

Take five minutes to explore any key reflections from the last session.

> Then he said to them all: 'If anyone would come after me, he must deny himself and take up his cross daily and follow me. For whoever wants to save his life will lose it, but whoever loses his life for me will save it.' (Luke 9:23–4)

A Story

I couldn't quite get my head around what my friend was saying. He was a young, hard-working professional engineer with an emerging business acumen. Having bought their first family home on a new, upwardly mobile estate, he ran into trouble when the economic slump in the late 1980s overtook him and his circumstances. He said he was in negative equity. In other words, what he was paying for his house exceeded its value, meaning that his property was worth nothing.

It took an awful lot of courage, diligence and faith for him to keep going against the odds, and to come out the other end without giving in to depression and losing his way. Today he is a successful businessman.

Encounter with Jesus: Luke 19:1–10

> Jesus entered Jericho and was passing through. A man was there by the name of Zacchaeus; he was a chief tax collector and was wealthy. He wanted to see who Jesus was, but being a short man he could not, because of the crowd. So he ran ahead and climbed a sycamore-fig tree to see him, since Jesus was coming that way.
>
> When Jesus reached the spot, he looked up and said to him, 'Zacchaeus, come down immediately. I must stay at your house today.' So he came down at once and welcomed him gladly.

> All the people saw this and began to mutter, 'He has gone to be the guest of a "sinner".'
>
> But Zacchaeus stood up and said to the Lord, 'Look, Lord! Here and now I give half of my possessions to the poor, and if I have cheated anybody out of anything, I will pay back four times the amount.'
>
> Jesus said to him, 'Today salvation has come to this house, because this man, too, is a son of Abraham. For the Son of Man came to seek and to save what was lost.'

On His journey to Jerusalem Jesus entered the town of Jericho. This would be Jesus' final trip to Jericho, because He was on His way to the cross. As the crowds gathered around to touch and be taught by Him, one individual had a particular problem. His name was Zacchaeus and he wasn't very tall. But he had an even bigger problem: as a tax collector he had amassed a lot of money, but had very few friends.

Tax collectors lived in social no-go areas. The Roman government ruled with an iron fist and collected taxes from the occupied regions to keep their power intact. And it wasn't just that they were a military power: they were also a pagan government who ensured that no religion eclipsed the Roman gods or the might of Rome. Anyone who collected taxes from Jews to pay their oppressor was in difficult territory to start with.

With all that in mind, the easiest way for a rejected man to take retribution was by charging commissions at a high rate of pay. The extortion was an act of revenge as much as an act of greed.

Rather than shying away from the crowds, however, Zacchaeus threw himself into the heart of the commotion and made himself quite conspicuous by climbing up a tree. He may well have had company in the tree, but oddly, Jesus spotted him and called him specifically to come down. And to everyone's amazement, Jesus was inviting Himself to the man's house for tea! Of all the people in all the trees in all of Jericho, Jesus chose a Roman collaborator and social outcast – a man with money, provincial influence, status and no social capital.

The social misfit dashed down from his perch and rushed off with Jesus towards his house. And without any promptings from Jesus, he made a public promise to give away at least half of his wealth to the poor and in addition to refund by 400 per cent any money taken by extortion! The encounter with Jesus transformed Zacchaeus from a social reject to the centre of attention and a moral giant.

In the presence of Jesus, Zacchaeus knew intuitively that you can own a lot and work a lot and still have nothing. Negative equity. In the presence of Jesus, he looked into a mirror and saw the emptiness of his own soul. But more than that, he discovered a practical way to fill that emptiness. He had to de-clutter.

What happened to him was seismic! In a moment of recognition, Zacchaeus the legalised thief had a values revolution. He saw for the first time that the things he possessed stood in the way of the relationships he might have had. He realised that money, power and influence can be a social burden even when they seem like economic advantage.

So, Jesus said, today we put the balance right, for 'salvation has come to this house'.

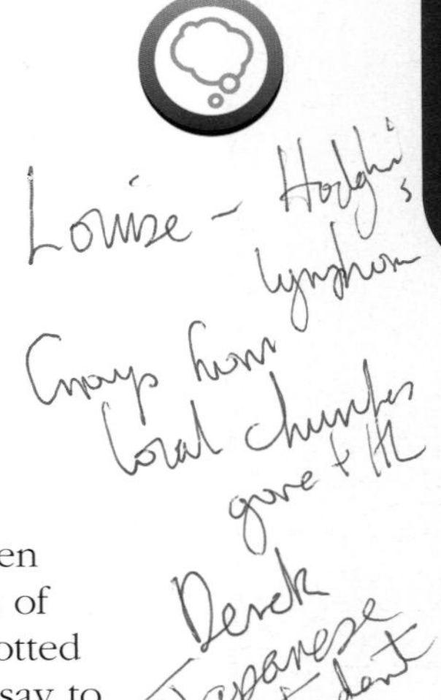

Reflections from Psalm 51:4-6

Against you, you only, have I sinned
and done what is evil in your sight,
so that you are proved *right when you speak*
and justified when *you judge.*
Surely I was sinful at birth,
sinful from the time my mother conceived me.
Surely you desire truth in the inner parts;
you teach me wisdom in the inmost place.

Something about Jesus jumped out at Zacchaeus when he met with Him. Although they were in the middle of a heaving crowd, it was as though this encounter blotted out everybody else. What do the highlighted words say to us as we live in relationships and yet seek to balance our lives and values?

Application

Our lives can be filled with activity which causes us to lose our way. We feel ourselves working hard with nothing much to show for it and all our effort is spent running fast in order to stand still. We invest time and effort which doesn't pay off and feel as though we dig holes merely to fill them in again.

It's not that we aren't doing interesting and exciting things, enjoying our annual holidays and holding down a good job: it's just that when our life is put on the scales, it doesn't really add up to anything more than the sum total of our activities.

In today's world, where people have become what they do rather than who they are, the easiest thing is to fall into negative equity and run our lives as though everything depends on what we have. But as our world continues to experience and reflect on the worst financial downturn in over fifty years, we have an opportunity to remind people around us that we are more than we own and that it really is possible to gain the whole world and lose our soul – the heart of who God has made us to become.

The offer which Jesus brings to the twenty-first century is more than the possibility of a final balance sheet in heaven; it is also the chance to live in the here and now in such a way that allows us to live life in all its abundance. The freedom from sin which Jesus offers is therefore the recognition that we can live surplus lives even amongst the real and awful demands of the economic challenges which face us on a daily basis.

We all want this quality of living. Little wonder that increasingly people are seeking out voluntary work or going off on spiritual retreats. It's as St Augustine said: 'Our souls are restless until we find our rest in Thee.' It's another way of describing the negative equity of lives detached from God.

A To-Do Moment!

Take a moment to make a note of anything the Lord may be saying to you about your response to what you have discovered about Him and your relationship to Him.

Jesus – A Quick Response: Luke 12:15

'Watch out! Be on your guard against all kinds of greed; a man's life does not consist in the abundance of his possessions.'

Discussion Starters

1. Imagine you are Zacchaeus: What might have been the first thoughts in your head when Jesus looked up at you in the tree? And what made you decide to give so much away?

2. Imagine you are Mrs Zacchaeus: What would your attitude have been to this big decision and how would it change your life and the family's life by proxy? Would you have needed convincing?

3. Imagine you are one of the people to receive money back from Zacchaeus: What does that make you think about Jesus, and what does it make you think about Zacchaeus now?

4. How would you react if Jesus invited Himself to your home today? What would that mean for you?

5. What are your priorities in life? Take a moment to make an honest list. Is there anything you would like to change, and how might you do that?

6. What do you understand by the phrase 'life in abundance'?

* What do we do to attract the outsiders? John's story ~ boys in school + church service

A Prayer

Lord Jesus,
We come to You, our all-sufficient Christ.
Take away from us the things which clutter and cripple
Your life in us.
Take away our greed;
Our selfish wants and wearying ambitions.
Release us from the stranglehold of things we own or the
gifts which You have given.
And free us to love and serve and share.
And fill us with Your life that we might really live.
So that in being owned by You
We might own all things.
Amen.

Jesus and Pollution

Retracing Our Steps

Take five minutes to explore any key reflections from the last session.

> The LORD smelled the pleasing aroma and said in his heart: 'Never again will I curse the ground because of man, even though every inclination of his heart is evil from childhood.' (Genesis 8:21)

A Story

My wife and I went on a one-week holiday to Gambia some years ago. This was our first trip to Africa and we were quite excited about it. When we woke the morning after our late arrival, high on our priority was a trip to the beach a few yards away from our hotel. So, after breakfast, we took a stroll to do our beach surveillance. When we got there we were shocked. What appeared in the brochures as an expanse of white sand was little more than a sulphur-ridden landscape. The beach had been ravaged by soil erosion.

We have come a long way since the days when our greatest pollutants were the steam trains and the house chimney. Today's pollutants are invisibly putting a stranglehold on our clean air supplies and breathing death over our rivers, oceans and lakes. Pollution is quietly destroying our unique species of sea life and something like 80 per cent of our forests.

Most of us stand in utter confusion as politicians, scientists and environmentalists have technical arguments about statistics, the rate of degradation and even who is responsible. But no one is arguing with the fact that pollution is happening with catastrophic effects on our environment, and that this will mean massive changes in the way we consume natural fuels and use energy.

Industrial plants which belch metric tonnes of fumes into the skies still provide us with graphic visuals of what pollution looks like. But the truth is that it is mostly invisible. The impact is far more powerful than the images. And, what's worse, pollution and progress make perfect bedfellows. The 747 jet which powders the skies with fumes as it rushes us across the world at 500 mph is just as culpable as those industrial plants.

As we all know, pollution doesn't need passports or visas. Few things have demonstrated our interdependence as a global village so clearly as our global markets and our pollution.

When the nuclear reactor in Chernobyl blew up in the Soviet Union on 26 April 1986, the result was catastrophic. It affected people as far away as France, Germany and the UK. It cost over $500 billion and caused at least 56 direct deaths and an estimated 4,000 cancer deaths. Today Chernobyl is still off limits.

Encounter with Jesus: Matthew 15:1–20

Then some Pharisees and teachers of the law came to Jesus from Jerusalem and asked, 'Why do your disciples break the tradition of the elders? They don't wash their hands before they eat!'

Jesus replied, 'And why do you break the command of God for the sake of your tradition? For God said, "Honour your father and mother" and "Anyone who curses his father or mother must be put to death." But you say that if a man says to his father or mother, "Whatever help you might otherwise have received from me is a gift devoted to God," he is not to "honour his father" with it. Thus you nullify the word of God for the sake of your tradition. You hypocrites! Isaiah was right when he prophesied about you:

"These people honour me with their lips,
but their hearts are far from me.
They worship me in vain;
their teachings are but rules taught by men."'

Jesus called the crowd to him and said, 'Listen and understand. What goes into a man's mouth does not make him "unclean", but what comes out of his mouth, that is what makes him "unclean".'

Then the disciples came to him and asked, 'Do you know that the Pharisees were offended when they heard this?'

He replied, 'Every plant that my heavenly Father has not planted will be pulled up by the roots. Leave them; they are blind guides. If a blind man leads a blind man, both will fall into a pit.'

Peter said, 'Explain the parable to us.'

'Are you still so dull?' Jesus asked them. 'Don't you see that whatever enters the mouth goes into the stomach and then out of the body? But the things that come out of the mouth come from the heart, and these make a man "unclean". For out of the heart come evil thoughts, murder, adultery, sexual immorality, theft, false testimony, slander. These are what make a man "unclean"; but eating with unwashed hands does not make him "unclean".'

Jesus had an amazing ability to tip things upside down. So when the disciples were accused of failing to follow the Jewish laws of purification by not washing their hands, it led to a private discussion with His disciples.

They had lived all their lives thinking that God was more concerned with hygiene than holiness. They thought that not washing hands before eating would be a problem for God, but Jesus gave them another view altogether. Jesus differentiated between what we put into our physical bodies and what we produce in our spirit. He made it quite clear that moral and spiritual pollution is far more serious than what you put in your mouth.

This in no way depreciates the importance of the body! It wasn't as though Jesus was saying, 'Put anything you like in your body – it will be fine!' Throughout the Scriptures there is a healthy appreciation for the body, which is regarded as God's temple. Rather, Jesus was attempting to reorder their personal priorities and by extension to help all of us see something far more important: inner pollution has nothing to do with cultural or religious etiquette, or even physical hygiene. But there is a desecration of the human spirit which pollutes us on the inside before spilling out to pollute other people.

Jesus' private tuition with the disciples was an attempt to help them know what to look for, but also to liberate them from things which didn't matter as much as they first thought.

Reflections from Psalm 51:7–10

Cleanse me with hyssop, and I shall be clean;
wash me, and I shall be *whiter than snow.*
Let me hear joy and gladness;
let the bones you have crushed rejoice.
Hide your face from my sins
and blot out *all my iniquity.*
Create in me a pure heart, O God,
and renew a steadfast spirit within me.

There is something very comprehensive in the words highlighted. As we think about the work of the cross through Lent, is this comprehensive level of inner purity a reality, or just a nice idea?

Application

The parallels which exist between what the Bible calls 'sin' and the pollution which takes place in the material world should not be difficult to explain. The deforestation of the human spirit is all around for us to see, and its effects are shared across our relationships.

The pollution which takes place in the human spirit is just as insidious as the pollution in the material world. And it can happen in the name of progress with equal devastation. Everyone agrees that the recent financial crisis – the worst to hit the world for a generation – is the unavoidable result of the pollutant of human greed. Greedy bankers, financiers and political systems all colluded in a conspiracy of greed. But as consumers we also played our part in stockpiling greed with impatience as we borrowed money to buy luxuries we didn't need. The price paid has been a very heavy one for people in poor countries who had little to do with it.

The notion that our misdemeanours are always and forever entirely private makes nonsense of our claims to community and shared humanity. Human nature harbours a shared tendency to pollute because within us a kind of pollution has taken place. The Christian faith is quite unique in its claim that everyone, everywhere, has been polluted by sin and that the 'clean-up' exercise is possible only because of the death and resurrection of Jesus Christ.

The universal character of our fallen nature is central to the meaning of Lent. Lent is a reminder of our corporate fallenness; a reminder that everyone has come short of what God had in mind for human beings, and that restoration can only be through Jesus.

A To-Do Moment!

Take a moment to make a note of anything the Lord may be saying to you about your response to what you have discovered about Him and your relationship to Him.

Jesus – A Quick Response: Luke 6:45b

'For out of the overflow of his heart his mouth speaks.'

Discussion Starters

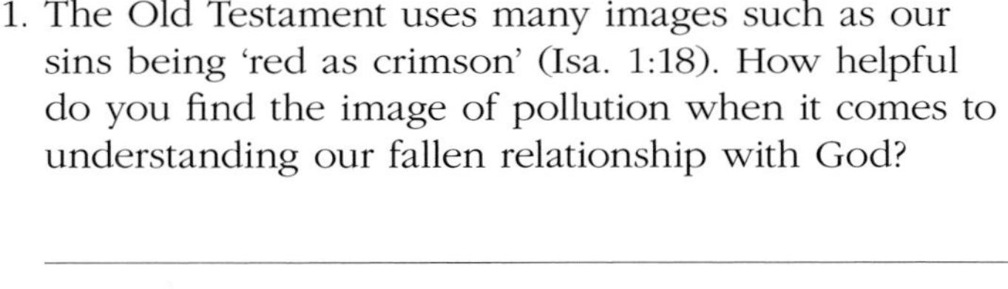

1. The Old Testament uses many images such as our sins being 'red as crimson' (Isa. 1:18). How helpful do you find the image of pollution when it comes to understanding our fallen relationship with God?

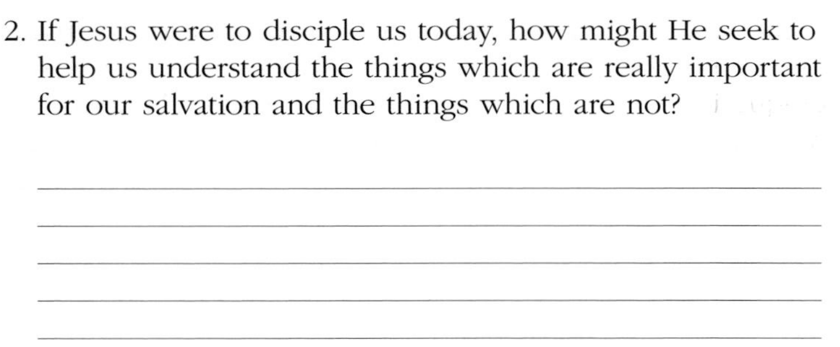

2. If Jesus were to disciple us today, how might He seek to help us understand the things which are really important for our salvation and the things which are not?

What rituals do we have for cleansing – one in particular similar to handwashing then? Baptism / Footwashing.

3. If you were in the encounter with Jesus described in the passage from Matthew, how easy would you find it to understand what He was saying?

4. How liberating do you find Jesus' teaching in this encounter?

5. Can you think of an incident when something you said or did had a negative impact on another person? What action, if any, can you take now to put the balance right?

Baptism?

6. 'I shall be whiter than snow.' What other images could you use to describe the cleansing, purifying work of God?

Ask two people to think through the material and come back next week with a summary of points from today's study. It doesn't have to be a three-point sermon! Just two or three minutes each capturing the key things for them.

A Prayer

Clean the slate, God, so we can start the day fresh!
    Keep me from stupid sins,
    from thinking I can take over your work;
Then I can start this day sun-washed,
    scrubbed clean of the grime of sin.
These are the words in my mouth;
    these are what I chew on and pray.

Psalm 19:13–14 (*The Message*)

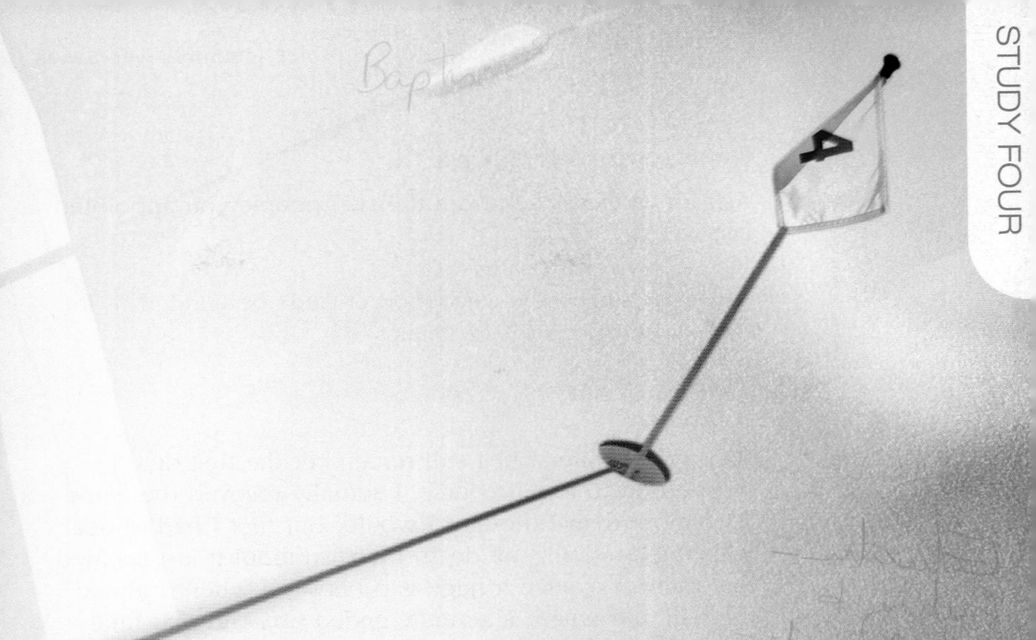

Jesus and People who Miss the Mark

Retracing our Steps

Ask for the feedback from the two people you appointed last week.

> All have sinned and come short of God's beautiful plans for our lives. (Romans 3:23, Phillips)

A Story

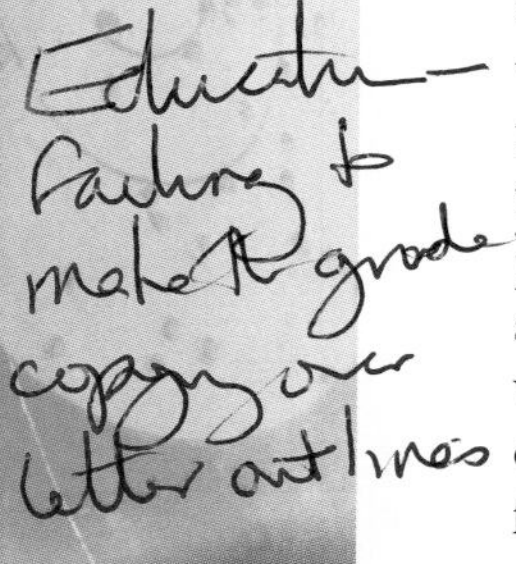

I am not a golfer, but I still remember the first time I stepped on to a golf course. I actually enjoyed the game a lot more than I thought I would. But first I had to deal with the possibility of death by frustration! It just seemed that there was such a huge gap between where I aimed the ball and where it actually ended up. And that final putt! How on earth you can miss when you're so near is something of a mystery to me. What makes it so much worse is that mental image every golfer has of the hole in one: that one perfect shot which lobs the golf ball directly from the tee into the hole.

Encounter with Jesus: Mark 10:17–25

As Jesus started on his way, a man ran up to him and fell on his knees before him. 'Good teacher,' he asked, 'what must I do to inherit eternal life?'

'Why do you call me good?' Jesus answered. 'No-one is good – except God alone. You know the commandments: "Do not murder, do not commit adultery, do not steal, do not give false testimony, do not defraud, honour your father and mother."'

'Teacher,' he declared, 'all these I have kept since I was a boy.'

Jesus looked at him and loved him. 'One thing you lack,' he said. 'Go, sell everything you have and give to the poor, and you will have treasure in heaven. Then come, follow me.'

> At this the man's face fell. He went away sad, because he had great wealth.
>
> Jesus looked around and said to his disciples, 'How hard it is for the rich to enter the kingdom of God!'
>
> The disciples were amazed at his words. But Jesus said again, 'Children, how hard it is to enter the kingdom of God! It is easier for a camel to go through the eye of a needle than for a rich man to enter the kingdom of God.'

When the wealthy young man came to Jesus, he was already eager to know about eternal life. So Jesus reminded him of the moral demands of the commandments. But the young man said he had been following those since he was a boy. Then Jesus looked at him and told him what he didn't want to hear. It was that he only lacked 'one thing'. He needed to sell everything which was holding him back, give it away to the poor, and follow Jesus.

But the rich man's 'one thing' was a very big thing. It wasn't just the money. There was no general or sweeping condemnation of wealth. As Martin Luther King once said, on this occasion Jesus was prescribing individual surgery rather than setting out a universal cure. If you don't have much money, it's easy to conclude that having it makes you a sinner. But this is not necessarily the case. Money can be a blessing – or a curse. Everything depends on our attitude to what we have. We must own things without them owning us. I still find it spiritually exhilarating to meet with wealthy Christians who have dedicated themselves to being good stewards of all that God has given them. To see a wealthy person serving is far more inspiring than seeing the average Christian shrouded in material values and oblivious to the poor.

Our sin is not to have things: it's to allow things to own us.

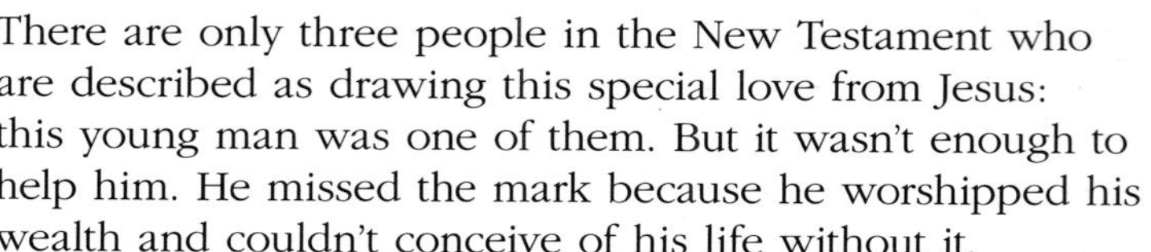

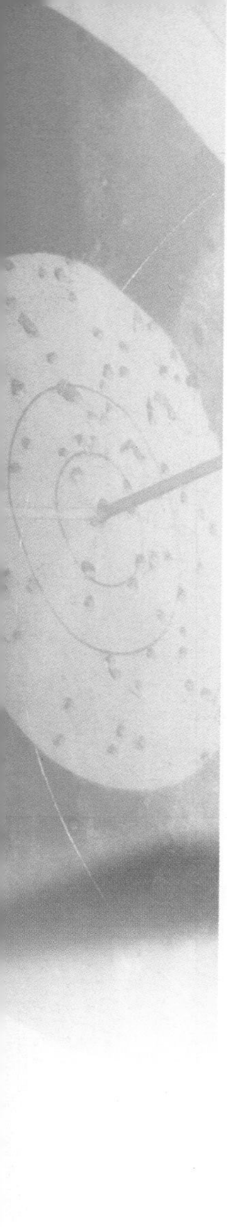

There are only three people in the New Testament who are described as drawing this special love from Jesus: this young man was one of them. But it wasn't enough to help him. He missed the mark because he worshipped his wealth and couldn't conceive of his life without it.

It was more serious than that, however. He couldn't bring himself to allow others less fortunate to benefit from it. His wealth had insulated him from the poor and his level of compassion was not sufficient to move him to use his wealth for other people's benefit.

This encounter with Jesus also reminds us of something else: not everyone who comes to Jesus and really wants to follow Him is prepared to bridge the gap between their desire to follow Him and what He demands of them. It reminds us too that we may never know what's *really* in our hearts or where our priorities are until we have an encounter with Jesus. This man would have gone through life sincerely believing that he was doing everything he needed to do in order to inherit eternal life. But when he met Jesus it became clear to him that sincerity is not enough to gain eternal life: you also need the courage to get your personal priorities right.

Jesus encounters us not to tell us what we want to hear, but to tell us what we need to know if we are to live as free people. In these encounters He acts as our life coach, pointing out the distance between God's plan for our lives and our desire to fulfil that plan.

What is really frightening is that He lets us choose.

Respectability about not doing things

Reflections from Psalm 51:11-13

Do not cast me from your presence
or take your Holy Spirit from me.
Restore to me the joy of your salvation
and grant me a willing spirit, to *sustain me*.
Then I will teach transgressors your ways,
and sinners will *turn back to you*.

Redemption is a great biblical truth. It stands at the very centre of Christ's work on the cross. How do the highlighted words help us to understand this idea of redemption for people who have missed the mark?

Application

There really is nothing more frustrating than missing the mark, especially when you are determined to be on target. This Lent, our world is filled with people who keep missing, and often it's not for lack of trying. All of us know what it means to put our very best effort forward, only to be met with the aching frustration of lives which fall short of our own ambitions for ourselves.

We know too of the utter desperation which comes with failing to be what we were meant to be as people made in God's image and for whom Jesus died. When St Paul tells us that 'all have sinned and fall short of the glory of God' (Rom. 3:23), this is precisely what he means. In fact, the word Paul uses here is drawn from the sports field and it means 'to miss the mark'. In this regard, it really doesn't matter whether we miss by a mile or a metre: the disappointment can be just as acute.

If you have ever played golf, you will know the truth in the claim that you're really playing against yourself as much as your opponent. Each of us has our own sense of accountability before God. Our task is not to point out other people's performances and to justify ourselves

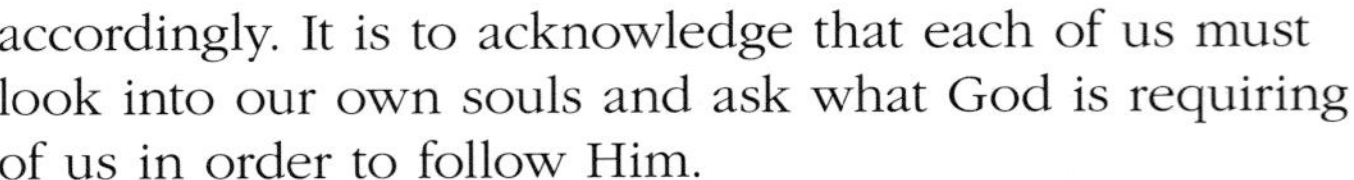

accordingly. It is to acknowledge that each of us must look into our own souls and ask what God is requiring of us in order to follow Him.

As far as the Bible is concerned, no one on the course has any room to gloat: we have all missed the mark, and we continue to miss the mark. Many of us strive to make up the loss in a thousand ways which often fail to bring fulfilment.

A To-Do Moment!

Take a moment to make a note of anything the Lord may be saying to you about your response to what you have discovered about Him and your relationship to Him.

Jesus – A Quick Response: John 10:10

'I have come that they may have life, and have it to the full.'

What commandments are missed out?

Discussion Starters

1. How is it possible for just 'one thing' to allow us to miss the mark?
   Can you identify a particular stumbling block in your own life at present?

2. This Lent many of us will talk to others about missing the mark. How do we persuade people about Jesus and also allow them to choose Him?

3. How would you explain the difference between 'the letter of the law' and 'the spirit of the law'?

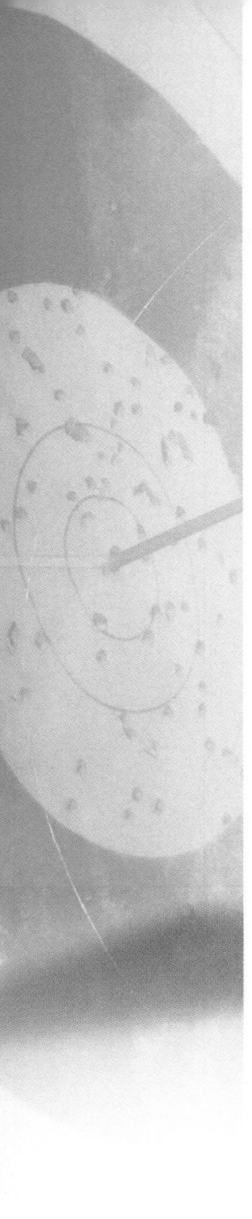

4. Is it really true that it's hard for a rich person to enter the kingdom of God, or is it just a saying we don't quite understand?

5. Do you see money/material possessions as a burden or an opportunity?

6. Do you believe that God has a plan for your life? Can you share with the group what you think that might mean? How might you follow His plan more closely?

A Prayer

O Lord early in the morning I cry to You. Help me to pray and to concentrate my thoughts on You: I cannot do this alone.
In me there is darkness. But with You there is light; I am lonely but You do not leave me; I am feeble in heart, but with You there is help; I am restless but with You there is peace. In me there is bitterness but with You there is patience; I do not understand Your ways, but You know the way for me. Restore me to liberty, and enable me so to live now that I may answer before men. Lord, whatever this day may bring, Your name be praised. Amen.

Dietrich Bonhoeffer, 1906–45, prayer written in prison while he awaited execution

STUDY FIVE

Jesus and a Blind Spot

Retracing our Steps

Take five minutes to explore any key reflections from the last session.

> Why do you look at the speck of sawdust in your brother's eye and pay no attention to the plank in your own eye? (Matthew 7:3)

A Story

If you're a driver, it's probably happened to you:

It was a great day for driving: blue skies, a relatively clear road and a steady flow on the motorway. As I approached the vehicle in front of me, I did everything right. I checked my rear mirror, indicated to turn out into the overtaking lane and made a final glance at the wing mirrors. All clear. But then, just as I assumed it was clear to pull out and was in the process of changing lane, I looked over my right shoulder to see the oncoming vehicle flashing past and the driver shaking his head in disapproving disbelief. And with the drama of that moment and the shaking limbs that resulted, I understood what we mean when we talk about a 'blind spot'.

You may be able to think of numerous and less life-threatening examples. Take, for instance, the time when someone pointed out that you were about to leave the house with breakfast on your chin and saved you from devastating embarrassment.

Encounter with Jesus: John 3:1–15 (also John 9:1–41)

> Now there was a man of the Pharisees named Nicodemus, a member of the Jewish ruling council. He came to Jesus at night and said, 'Rabbi, we know you are a teacher who has

come from God. For no-one could perform the miraculous signs you are doing if God were not with him.'
In reply Jesus declared, 'I tell you the truth, no-one can see the kingdom of God unless he is born again.'

'How can a man be born when he is old?' Nicodemus asked. 'Surely he cannot enter a second time into his mother's womb to be born!'

Jesus answered, 'I tell you the truth, no-one can enter the kingdom of God unless he is born of water and the Spirit. Flesh gives birth to flesh, but the Spirit gives birth to spirit. You should not be surprised at my saying, "You must be born again." The wind blows wherever it pleases. You hear its sound, but you cannot tell where it comes from or where it is going. So it is with everyone born of the Spirit.'

'How can this be?' Nicodemus asked.

'You are Israel's teacher,' said Jesus, 'and do you not understand these things? I tell you the truth, we speak of what we know, and we testify to what we have seen, but still you people do not accept our testimony. I have spoken to you of earthly things and you do not believe; how then will you believe if I speak of heavenly things? No-one has ever gone into heaven except the one who came from heaven – the Son of Man. Just as Moses lifted up the snake in the desert, so the Son of Man must be lifted up, that everyone who believes in him may have eternal life.'

In the early stages of Jesus' ministry, a senior rabbi named Nicodemus sought out Jesus for a chat. Intuitively he knew he had a blind spot. He had seen and heard things in Jesus' work which were totally unfamiliar to him: things which even went against all his theological instincts. He had blind spots and he knew it.

Under the cloak of night, this very clever and senior leader came to see Jesus to talk about things he didn't understand. He wanted to know how it was that Jesus did such amazing miracles. So Jesus explained that the only people who could see God's kingdom were the ones who had a second birth. Nicodemus couldn't see the point. Teacher though he was, he couldn't get past the absurdity of an old man unlearning all he knew about God and being born all over again. He was really sincere, but we don't know if he ever really saw the kingdom of God.

There was also another man who was physically blind and who was later enabled to see. In fact, this man was born blind and became the butt of controversy. Religious leaders wanted to know if his or his parents' sin was responsible for his blindness. But after Jesus daubed mud on his eyes and sent him staggering off to wash in a nearby pool, the man came back seeing. It wasn't just that he could now see physically: this man was now able to see Jesus as the Son of Man.

There were, however, those whose blindness led to spiritual obstinacy. Jesus said that He had come into the world so that 'the blind will see and those who see will become blind' (John 9:39). He said that because His real difficulty was with those who were so blind that they couldn't see it. Blind spots can act like spiritual black holes which lock us for ever into unforgiveness.

Two readings – one where a blind spot is recognised, + one where not.

Reflections from Psalm 51:14–15

> Save me from bloodguilt, O God,
> the God who saves me,
> and my tongue will sing of your righteousness.
> *O Lord, open my lips,*
> and my mouth will declare your praise.

What do you make of this unusual phrase? Surely it's up to us to open our own lips in order to praise God? Or might it point to something else which God has to do in order to open us up?

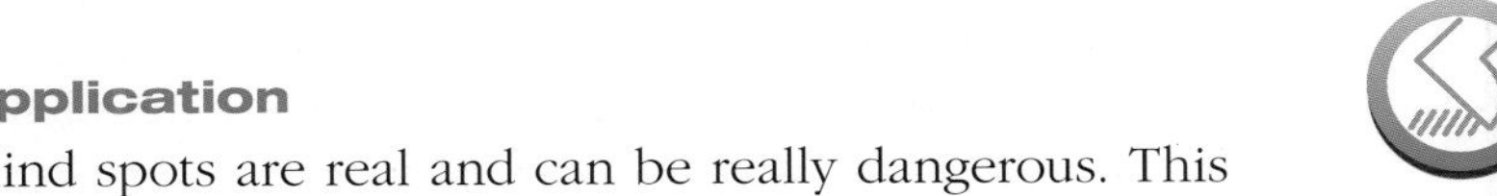

Application

Blind spots are real and can be really dangerous. This is because we can only act on what we see. If we all stood still until we knew everything which can be known about everything, we would all do nothing. So most of us step out in life on the basis of what we know and look to others to help us identify our blind spots. In part, maturity and proper self-adjustment is the ability to realise that we have blind spots which put us at risk. Secure people are OK with asking other people to tell them when they are about to make a spectacle of themselves.

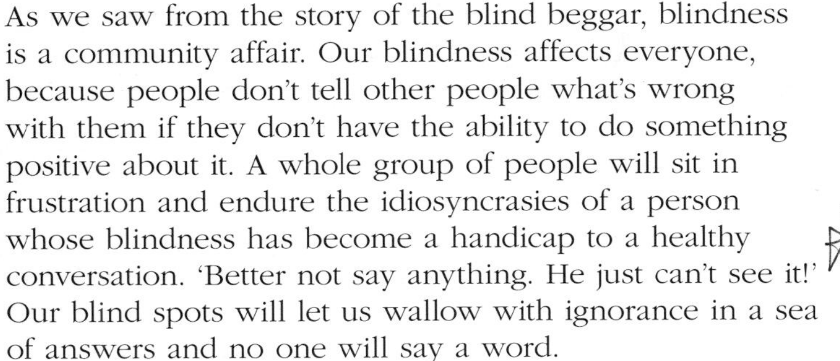

As we saw from the story of the blind beggar, blindness is a community affair. Our blindness affects everyone, because people don't tell other people what's wrong with them if they don't have the ability to do something positive about it. A whole group of people will sit in frustration and endure the idiosyncrasies of a person whose blindness has become a handicap to a healthy conversation. 'Better not say anything. He just can't see it!' Our blind spots will let us wallow with ignorance in a sea of answers and no one will say a word.

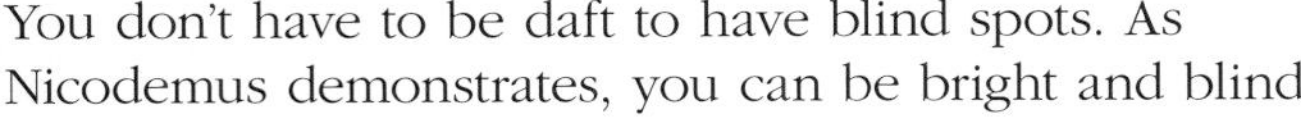

You don't have to be daft to have blind spots. As Nicodemus demonstrates, you can be bright and blind.

Some of the most skilful drivers run into trouble with blind spots. Too often we run into the hazards of our blind spots simply because we refuse to believe that they exist in our lives, or that anyone else can help us look out for them. We know we are in serious trouble with our blind spots when we miss our own and spend our lives pointing out everyone else's. An obsession with other people's weaknesses or sadnesses may therefore be the most certain signal that my blind spot is a universe of danger in which I am happily bumping into one disaster after another. And none of them, of course, is my fault. So we go through life with little to be sorry for and feeling that there's a lot to be sore about. Our blindness makes it impossible to see what's wrong with us and magnifies what's not quite right in other people.

It takes a mature person to see that he or she is blind.

Our spiritual blindness doesn't take away our faculties or even our brilliance. It hides God from us and makes us vulnerable. There are few ironies in life greater than the brilliance which blinds us to God. For in that blindness our pride makes us apt to grope in the dark instead of grabbing on to God. This blind spot has been the province of many brilliant minds who are content that there is no greater light and no better life than that which they can provide for themselves, and no concept of guilt which should lead us to a Saviour. As Sigmund Freud famously taught us, there is no such thing as guilt, only 'a sense of guilt'. Guilt without God needs no forgiveness and a sense of guilt has no need of a Saviour.

Guilt without God or the need of a Saviour is the ultimate wreckage: for there is no forgiveness when we cannot see our own blindness.

A To-Do Moment!

Take a moment to make a note of anything the Lord may be saying to you about your response to what you have discovered about Him and your relationship to Him.

Jesus – A Quick Response: John 9:37

'You have now seen him; in fact, he is the one speaking with you.'

Discussion Starters

1. Can you share with the group a 'blind spot' story? Have you had a near miss? (These stories may be humorous or quite tragic, so it may be time for group sensitivity or even prayer.)

Get told something you

all along.

2. What stops us from being up front about our blind spots, and how might we support each other in this?

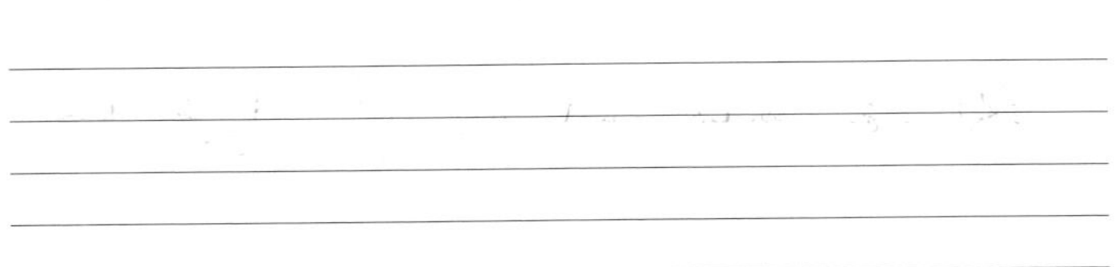

3. Talking about sin as 'spiritual blindness' can actually come across as Christian arrogance. Can we avoid that, and if so, how?
   If we can't, what do we do about it?

   If we always use it to refer to other people's!

4. What do you make of Jesus' attitude to Nicodemus? Could He have been less obscure and helped Nicodemus into the kingdom with a clearer answer?

5. Compare Jesus' response to the blind man, who didn't ask for help, with His response to Nicodemus, who came seeking answers. How do these two responses differ and what are we to make of Jesus' methods in both cases?

   Blind man not curious about 'how'

6. 'I feel so guilty …' What might you say to lead someone who feels a sense of guilt to accept the need for personal forgiveness from God?

A Prayer

God be in my head, and in my understanding;
God be in my eyes, and in my looking;
God be in my mouth and in my speaking;
God be in my heart and in my thinking;
God be in my end, and at my departing.

Sarum Primer, 1558

100% COTTON
L

Jesus and Slavery

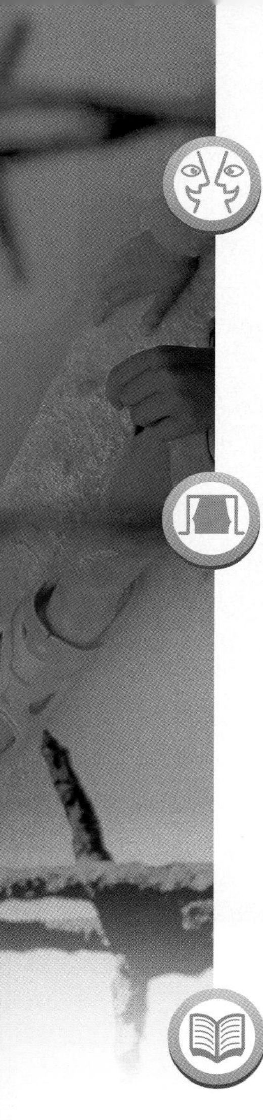

Retracing Our Steps

Take five minutes to explore any key reflections from the last session.

> The LORD said, 'I have indeed seen the misery of my people in Egypt. I have heard them crying out because of their slave drivers, and I am concerned about their suffering.' (Exodus 3:7)

A Story

In February 2007 a packed congregation met at Westminster Abbey to celebrate the bicentenary of the abolition of the slave trade. As we remembered the past atrocities of the killing of some 20 million Africans in the transatlantic slave trade, we also paused to remember and regret the 20 million twenty-first-century slaves today.

Those of us who live in democracies find it difficult to grasp the fact that slavery still exists. In today's world there are over 218 million child labourers and over a million children who are being trafficked every year. We find it incredible that, given our love for freedom, some people can dehumanise other people for money and power.

Encounter with Jesus: Mark 5:1–20

> They went across the lake to the region of the Gerasenes. When Jesus got out of the boat, a man with an evil spirit came from the tombs to meet him. This man lived in the tombs, and no-one could bind him any more, not even with a chain. For he had often been chained hand and foot, but he tore the chains apart and broke the irons on his feet. No-one was strong enough to subdue him. Night and day among the tombs and in the hills he would cry out and cut himself with stones.

When he saw Jesus from a distance, he ran and fell on his knees in front of him. He shouted at the top of his voice, 'What do you want with me, Jesus, Son of the Most High God? Swear to God that you won't torture me!' For Jesus had said to him, 'Come out of this man, you evil spirit!'

Then Jesus asked him, 'What is your name?'

'My name is Legion,' he replied, 'for we are many.' And he begged Jesus again and again not to send them out of the area.

A large herd of pigs was feeding on the nearby hillside. The demons begged Jesus, 'Send us among the pigs; allow us to go into them.' He gave them permission, and the evil spirits came out and went into the pigs. The herd, about two thousand in number, rushed down the steep bank into the lake and were drowned.

Those tending the pigs ran off and reported this in the town and countryside, and the people went out to see what had happened. When they came to Jesus, they saw the man who had been possessed by the legion of demons, sitting there, dressed and in his right mind; and they were afraid. Those who had seen it told the people what had happened to the demon-possessed man – and told about the pigs as well. Then the people began to plead with Jesus to leave their region.

As Jesus was getting into the boat, the man who had been demon-possessed begged to go with him. Jesus did not let him, but said, 'Go home to your family and tell them how much the Lord has done for you, and how he has had mercy on you.' So the man went away and began to tell in the Decapolis how much Jesus had done for him. And all the people were amazed.

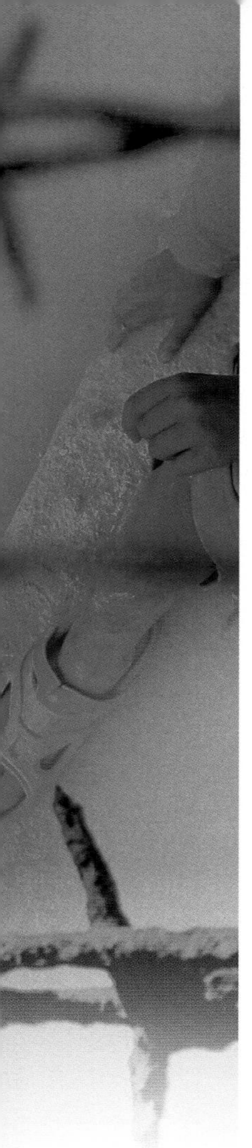

Jesus had many dramatic encounters, but perhaps few were as dramatic or even as frightening as His meeting with this demonic man. It was like going from one storm to another as Jesus and His disciples left the storm-tossed sea and disembarked on the south side of the Sea of Galilee.

As He stepped out of the boat, a man emerged from the nearby tombs where he lived and rushed at Jesus, protesting as he came. He was a frightening sight. As strong as an ox, no one could control him. He was a self-abuser who cut himself day and night and at any time people could hear him screaming in the hills and amongst the tombstones. He was literally tormented; Jesus had met no one as disturbed as this man.

The encounter was a combination of dialogue and deliverance.

The evil mastery in the man begged Jesus not to destroy them and appealed for alternative accommodation in a herd of pigs nearby. When Jesus changed their location from the man to the pigs, the whole herd crashed into the lake.

But the whole point of the story was that the man was transformed! A man who was bullied and tormented by evil was free. He was in his right mind and looked like another person altogether. Before he *did* anything different people already knew he *was* different. The abolition of slavery.

Oddly, the people around seemed more worried about what had happened on the hillside than they were about the state of the man when he was in bondage. And they weren't particularly pleased about their floating pigs.

The encounter was so powerful and the man's freedom so thorough that he wanted to leave the city to follow Jesus. But Jesus told him to stay and tell his story in the ten cities of the region.

Reflections from Psalm 51:16-19

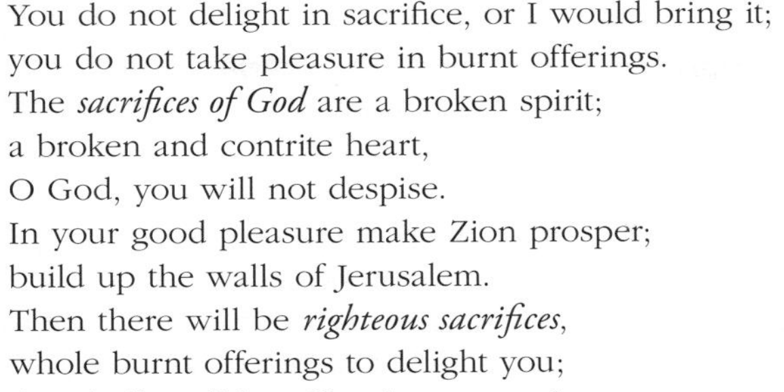

You do not delight in sacrifice, or I would bring it;
you do not take pleasure in burnt offerings.
The *sacrifices of God* are a broken spirit;
a broken and contrite heart,
O God, you will not despise.
In your good pleasure make Zion prosper;
build up the walls of Jerusalem.
Then there will be *righteous sacrifices*,
whole burnt offerings to delight you;
then bulls will be offered on your altar.

We always think of Lent as a time of sacrifice. How does this passage guide our thoughts about sacrifices this Lent?

Application

What makes slavery so awful is the diminishing of the image of God in people's lives. But it's also the mastery which someone else has over another human being.

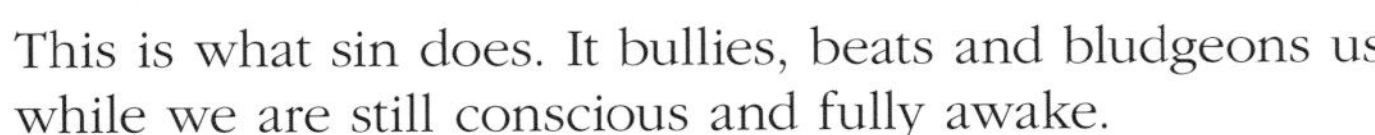

This is what sin does. It bullies, beats and bludgeons us while we are still conscious and fully awake.

Those of us who work in the judicial system will come across this time and again as we meet men and women – young and old – whose lives are controlled either by substance abuse or the culture of offending which dominates their lives, controls the range of their relationships and lands them in a prison cell again and again.

Slavery to sin is not always that dramatic, however. It is just as powerful when it invades our sexuality and locks us into private compulsions from which we are desperate to escape.

Nothing presents us with as powerful an image of sin and sinfulness as the reality of our own internal slavery. And

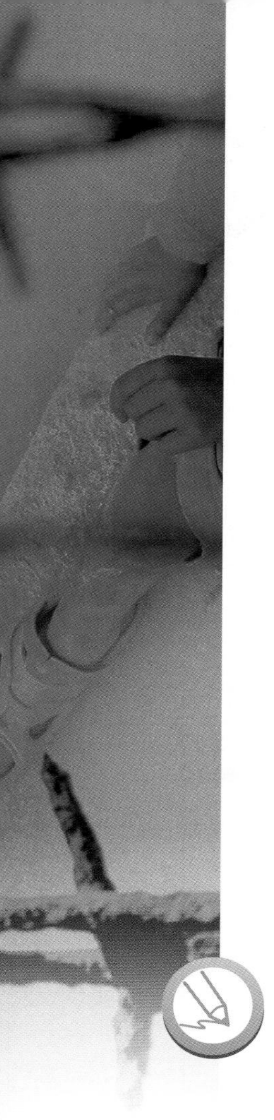

nothing is more liberating than Christ's willingness and power to free us from the things which hold us in slavery and chain us to the people we would rather not be. Lent and the cross of Christ celebrate the abolition of the slavery to sin.

That freedom has a benevolent purpose. As Paul reminded us, 'It is for freedom that Christ has set us free' (Gal. 5:1), and this freedom is at its very best when we realise that our liberty is meant to bring others into freedom. The most celebrated slave of the eighteenth century was Olaudah Equiano, who was baptised at St Margaret's Church, Westminster in 1757 and later obtained his freedom in 1766. What also brought him to public attention was the fact that he later became closely involved in the movement for the abolition of the slave trade, working with noted figures such as Granville Sharpe and many others as forerunners for William Wilberforce.

The same is true for us today. Christ sets us free to pray and work for the freedom of others. We are free to serve.

A To-Do Moment!

Take a moment to make a note of anything the Lord may be saying to you about your response to what you have discovered about Him and your relationship to Him.

Jesus – A Quick Response: John 8:36

'So if the Son sets you free, you will be free indeed.'

Discussion Starters

1. What do you understand from the phrase 'free to serve'? What does it mean to you personally?

2. What freedoms do you have to celebrate and thank God for in your own life?

3. Take some time to review these six sessions. Identify two or three key things you have learned:

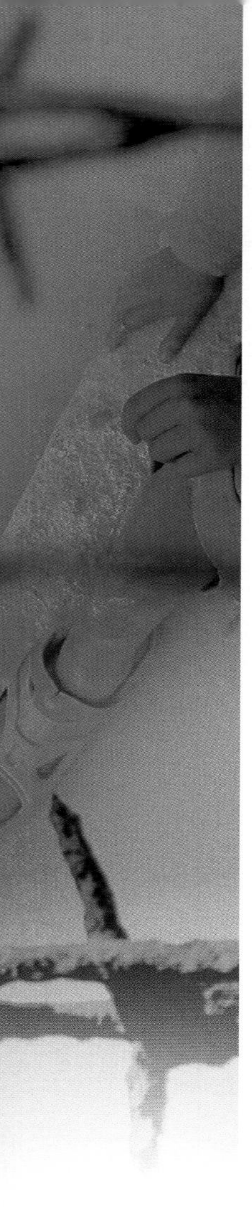

4. Is there a particular biblical idea you will want to follow up in the future?

5. Can you identify two things you will try to put into action?

6. Which, if any, of these six studies has spoken to you most significantly?

A Prayer

We are no longer our own, but Yours.
Put us to what You will, rank us with whom You will;
put us to doing, put us to suffering;
let us be employed for You or laid aside for You,
exalted for You or brought low for You;
let us be full, let us be empty;
let us have all things, let us have nothing.
We freely and wholeheartedly yield all things to Your
pleasure and disposal.
And now glorious and blessed God,
Father, Son and Holy Spirit,
You are ours and we are Yours.
So be it.
And the covenant which we made on earth,
let it be ratified in heaven.

Adapted from the Methodist Covenant Prayer

Leader's Notes

Study One: Jesus and Bad Stuff

All six sessions are trying to help us do one thing: to embrace the reality of sin and yet to find creative ways in which to relate this old idea to the Person and work of Christ and the meaning of Lent.

The *Story* starting off this study on sin with reference to a child's experience is rather intentional. The idea of sin can be either abstract or wholly condemning, but usually a child tends to be neither of these. It's also important to note that each of our lessons will begin with a brief story. This enables us to get inside the everyday-ness of our fallen nature. But it also helps us to think together about how the enormity of the idea of sin really has to become translated into the world in which we live. This is the point of our study.

The *Encounter with Jesus* picks up on Saul's incredible experience. Try to step back into Saul's head. On the road to Damascus we meet Saul of Tarsus, *not* Paul the apostle. What he experienced was a radical and terrifying meeting and the recognition that you can be on the right road going in the wrong direction. Try to help the group engage with the enormity of this change of mind.

You will notice that each encounter has Christ at its centre, reacting with different individuals in order to illustrate the theme. Try to keep in mind that although the characters will change, Christ remains the central character. In our studies, neither the theme nor the various characters should overshadow the Person of Christ.

The *Psalm* provides an Old Testament contrast with our New Testament story. As far as possible, it tries to mirror the central message of the encounter with Jesus. See how far you can help the group to balance the substance of the study with the key ideas which emerge from Psalm 51:1–3. Even though some key words are highlighted to provide focus, don't be afraid to hear what the Holy Spirit may be saying about the rest of the passage.

The *Application* brings us back to our own stories. Try to guide people to make the bridge between Saul's 'bad stuff' and our own 'bad stuff'. Using a child's description of 'bad stuff' is not meant to trivialise the issue, but neither is it meant to trap us in guilt. Help the group to recognise that Jesus meets us with our bad stuff not to condemn us, but, as with Saul, to send us in a new direction.

A To-Do Moment! Every study will give an opportunity to be practical about what God has been saying to us. Try to give people time to take this seriously. Remember, it doesn't mean they have to leave the room with a fully worked-out strategy to change the world! But it is important to make the space to be practical.

The *Discussion Starters* give time for interaction, but do feel free to guide people in this. They may not need to work through all the questions. If people become very engaged in the first few questions, do not feel you have to push them along to the others.

A Prayer comes at the end. There are many ways to pray a short prayer. Do think imaginatively about this. It could be one person praying for everyone, or even two or three people taking a line each.

Study Two: Jesus and Negative Equity

This may be a rather unusual study – particularly if the whole business of finance is a somewhat foreign idea for you. So you may need to spend a little time ahead of the study to find out a bit more about the idea of negative equity.

The *Story* here is seasonal, so as we come to this study keep two things in mind. First, this is an illustration, not a lesson in economics or mortgage lending! Second, as we do this study, it is likely that in our recent global financial downturn this could well apply to members of your group. Do be sensitive and prayerful about this as you prepare.

Zacchaeus's *Encounter with Jesus* is an amazing story. Try to get into the head of a man who lived among people who didn't like him very much. And what was he doing up in the tree anyway? Did he want to see Jesus as he scrambled up the tree, or did he want to be seen?

The *Psalm* carries on with an opportunity for self-analysis. Help the group explore how this might have related to someone like Zacchaeus and, by inference, to ourselves. What the psalm does here is to show how what we do in robbing other people is ultimately still a matter which God deals with as behaviour against Himself.

In the *Application*, don't forget that the object of the exercise here is to help the group see what negative equity is in relation to how we measure value. Owning possessions without God's love and care for other people is a form of negative equity and a failure to be what God would have us be. This may also be an opportunity to help those who have been caught in the financial crisis to see themselves as still valuable to God. Who knows: it may even be possible for God to use this crisis to redirect people about their priorities and future work.

The *To-Do Moment* may therefore be quite life-changing for some people.

In the *Discussion Starters* the first three questions could be taken together as something of a creative/dramatic time. You may want to do something about it the week before: if you happen to have people in the group with drama skills or experience, you could invite them to prepare something in advance.

Study Three: Jesus and Pollution

This study has very close parallels to Study One on 'Bad Stuff'. The difference isn't huge, but if it helps, think of this study more as an exploration in how we display our sinfulness, the behaviour which comes as a result of our sinfulness and our reaction with others around us. The first study looks more deliberately at our nature of sinfulness.

The *Story* could generate a discussion about the environment. It's really important to acknowledge that this is a very important issue, but it's not what we are doing here. By all means, get people to follow through on the environment at a later stage; but for our study we are specifically trying to help the group to understand and talk about what Jesus has done for us in our sin and sinfulness.

Our *Encounter with Jesus* and *Application* show His ability to get on the inside of people's situations. The idea here is to help the group explore Jesus' priority with what is happening on the inside rather than the rituals we go through in church life. Here is an opportunity to make Him a living, relational and forgiving Christ – not just a tick-box teacher. How might this help the group to see

Jesus as someone who is profoundly concerned with what makes us tick rather than with what we do?

The *Psalm* gives us a before-and-after effect. The cleansing work of Christ makes fundamental changes in our lives. If you have an opportunity to show snapshots of a before-and-after effect, that might help to make the point. It could be a photo of a polluted beach and a shot of what it looked like after it was restored. Or it might be photos of a renovated property.

With the *Discussion Starters*, don't feel you have to rush through all the questions. In fact, you may want to use some of the time to discuss who will follow through and bring back some thoughts the following week. As this is the third study, it may already be obvious who might be open to doing this, but it could also be good fun to have an interactive process to decide who gets the short straw!

Study Four: Jesus and People who Miss the Mark

It's very easy to come to this study with a sense of foreboding and failure. That is not the object of the exercise. It's far more important to show that in one way or another all of us have missed the mark on what God wants.

The *Story* may be helped along if you have a video or DVD of great sporting gaffes. Someone may know of a film or cartoon which has made the point very well. Perhaps the funnier the better! Once again, don't be afraid to get the group involved in finding and presenting the material. You may well be blessed with a golfer who has a recording of a near miss at the final hole!

The *Encounter with Jesus* is one of the saddest stories in the New Testament – a case of so near and yet so far. Try not to miss the point here: it wasn't the man's wealth which was the problem. Jesus found a man who wanted life, but whose wealth was in the way.

The *Psalm* attempts to focus on positive and redemptive possibilities. If people have missed God's plan, Christ has come to bring restoration. Try to guide people to recognise this.

The *Application* this week should really seek to bring an element of resolution for people who may have come to realise that at some point and in some way they have missed what God wanted for them. Don't allow people to escape into an anti-wealth posture. The more important issue here is that really good people can still miss the mark. And be aware of people in the group who may be in business or aspiring to become successful in business.

It's really important to give people time with the *To-Do Moment.*

The time for the *Discussion Starters* and the final *Prayer* is equally important. What may have begun as a light-hearted and humorous time together could be quite profound for people. The final prayer from Bonhoeffer could be very poignant. It may be useful to know a bit more about him. Why not Google him for a brief insight into his life and death and thoughts about discipleship? Don't forget: the idea is not to send people away feeling hopeless, but to finish on a positive note about how Christ can restore us to the place God had in mind for each of us.

Study Five: Jesus and a Blind Spot

It's likely that our *Story* will relate to many people in the group! Give a thought to how you might make good use of this as a conversation starter.

This *Encounter with Jesus* may be well known to many in the group. But you may want to explore how far Jesus really expected Nicodemus to know what He was talking about. Are blind spots 'natural spots'? If so, it's worth thinking of how much patience Jesus exercises in responding to each of us.

This lesson covers two cases of blindness. It would be good to explore how Jesus responds to both men and what lessons this has for us today in how we understand His dealings with us.

You may find that the *Psalm* extract doesn't fit into the study quite as previous ones have done. Feel free to let it speak to you and the group as it continues to take us on a journey of healing and cleansing.

Hopefully the *Application* will be very meaningful to many in the group. If our relationship with Jesus and redemption means anything for us in our human relationships, this part of our study must be one of the most pivotal for us. It's important to guide the group to understand how our willingness to see our own weakness is really important for our life in Christ.

Both the *To-Do Moment* and *Discussion Starters* could leave people feeling a little exposed, as they may touch on real-life relationships. It's really important to avoid making the session into an impromptu counselling group! The group will have come to know each other quite well by now, but if there are real needs which emerge, be sure to point people to further help and support if necessary.

Study Six: Jesus and Slavery

The *Story* of slavery can provoke deep-seated emotions. Given that this is our final study together, we want to ensure that we end on a positive note. But we are also in a world where this is a growing issue. In fact, some members of the group may be actively involved in some sort of anti-slavery or anti-trafficking movement. A personal insight from someone may help to lighten up the subject without losing its gravity. Once again, you may want to ask someone in advance to share their experience.

This *Encounter with Jesus* is dramatic and may even be controversial for some people within the group. For example, some may want to ask if people are still possessed by evil spirits today. But again, we mustn't allow the discussion to wander off into controversy about exorcism. The point is a liberating one: Christ has come to set us free from anything which stops us from experiencing life in the here and now. It would be great for the group to have a sense of freedom for mission, as was the case in this encounter.

In fact, the *Psalm*, *Application*, *To-Do Moment*, *Discussion Starters* and final *Prayer* are all pointing in that direction. A successful Lent course will be one which has given the group a vital encounter with the living Christ, who not only sets us free from our sin, but sets us free to help others encounter Him in their fallenness and failures.

National Distributors

UK: (and countries not listed below)
CWR, Waverley Abbey House, Waverley Lane, Farnham, Surrey GU9 8EP.
Tel: (01252) 784700 Outside UK (44) 1252 784700

AUSTRALIA: CMC Australasia, PO Box 519, Belmont, Victoria 3216.
Tel: (03) 5241 3288 Fax: (03) 5241 3290

CANADA: David C Cook Distribution Canada, PO Box 98, 55 Woodslee Avenue, Paris, Ontario N3L 3E5. Tel: 1800 263 2664

GHANA: Challenge Enterprises of Ghana, PO Box 5723, Accra.
Tel: (021) 222437/223249 Fax: (021) 226227

HONG KONG: Cross Communications Ltd, 1/F, 562A Nathan Road, Kowloon.
Tel: 2780 1188 Fax: 2770 6229

INDIA: Crystal Communications, 10-3-18/4/1, East Marredpalli, Secunderabad – 500026, Andhra Pradesh. Tel/Fax: (040) 27737145

KENYA: Keswick Books and Gifts Ltd, PO Box 10242-00400, Nairobi.
Tel: (254) 20 312639/3870125

MALAYSIA: Salvation Book Centre (M) Sdn Bhd, 23 Jalan SS 2/64, 47300 Petaling Jaya, Selangor. Tel: (03) 78766411/78766797 Fax: (03) 78757066/78756360

Canaanland, No. 25 Jalan PJU 1A/41B, NZX Commercial Centre, Ara Jaya, 47301 Petaling Jaya, Selangor. Tel: (03) 7885 0540/1/2 Fax: (03) 7885 0545

NEW ZEALAND: CMC Australasia, PO Box 303298, North Harbour, Auckland 0751.
Tel: 0800 449 408 Fax: 0800 449 049

NIGERIA: FBFM, Helen Baugh House, 96 St Finbarr's College Road, Akoka, Lagos.
Tel: (01) 7747429/4700218/825775/827264

PHILIPPINES: OMF Literature Inc, 776 Boni Avenue, Mandaluyong City.
Tel: (02) 531 2183 Fax: (02) 531 1960

SINGAPORE: Alby Commercial Enterprises Pte Ltd, 95 Kallang Avenue #04-00, AIS Industrial Building, 339420. Tel: (65) 629 27238 Fax: (65) 629 27235

SOUTH AFRICA: Struik Christian Books, 80 MacKenzie Street, PO Box 1144, Cape Town 8000. Tel: (021) 462 4360 Fax: (021) 461 3612

SRI LANKA: Christombu Publications (Pvt) Ltd, Bartleet House, 65 Braybrooke Place, Colombo 2. Tel: (9411) 2421073/2447665

USA: David C Cook Distribution Canada, PO Box 98, 55 Woodslee Avenue, Paris, Ontario N3L 3E5, Canada. Tel: 1800 263 2664

For email addresses, visit the CWR website: www.cwr.org.uk

CWR is a Registered Charity – Number 294387

CWR is a Limited Company registered in England – Registration Number 1990308

Also available in the bestselling *Cover to Cover Bible Study* Series

These unique resources for group and individual study feature seven stimulating 1- to 2-hour sessions featuring icebreakers, Scripture references, discussion starters, suggestions for personal application and leader's notes, making it easy for you to conduct Bible studies that impact people's lives.

1 Corinthians
Growing a Spirit-filled church
ISBN: 978-1-85345-374-8

1 Timothy
Healthy churches – effective Christians
ISBN: 978-1-85345-291-8

23rd Psalm
The Lord is my Shepherd
ISBN: 978-1-85345-449-3

2 Timothy and Titus
Vital Christianity
ISBN: 978-1-85345-338-0

Ecclesiastes
Hard questions and spiritual answers
ISBN: 978-1-85345-371-7

Ephesians
Claiming your inheritance
ISBN: 978-1-85345-229-1

Esther
For such a time as this
ISBN: 978-1-85345-511-7

Fruit of the Spirit
Growing more like Jesus
ISBN: 978-1-85345-375-5

Genesis 1–11
Foundations of reality
ISBN: 978-1-85345-404-2

God's Rescue Plan
Finding God's fingerprints on human history
ISBN: 978-1-85345-294-9

Great Prayers of the Bible
Applying them to our lives today
ISBN: 978-1-85345-253-6

Hebrews
Jesus – simply the best
ISBN: 978-1-85345-337-3

Hosea
The love that never fails
ISBN: 978-1-85345-290-1

Isaiah 1–39
Prophet to the nations
ISBN: 978-1-85345-510-0

James
Faith in action
ISBN: 978-1-85345-293-2

Jeremiah
The passionate prophet
ISBN: 978-1-85345-372-4

Joseph
The power of forgiveness and reconciliation
ISBN: 978-1-85345-252-9

Mark
Life as it is meant to be lived
ISBN: 978-1-85345-233-8

Moses
Face to face with God
ISBN: 978-1-85345-336-6

Nehemiah
Principles for life
ISBN: 978-1-85345-335-9

Parables
Communicating God on earth
ISBN: 978-1-85345-340-3

Philemon
From slavery to freedom
ISBN: 978-1-85345-453-0

Philippians
Living for the sake of the gospel
ISBN: 978-1-85345-421-9

Proverbs
Living a life of wisdom
ISBN: 978-1-85345-373-1

Revelation 1-3
Christ's call to the Church
ISBN: 978-1-85345-461-5

Revelation 4-22
The Lamb wins! Christ's final victory
ISBN: 978-1-85345-411-0

Rivers of Justice
Responding to God's call to righteousness today
ISBN: 978-1-85345-339-7

Ruth
Loving kindness in action
ISBN: 978-1-85345-231-4

The Covenants
God's promises and their relevance today
ISBN: 978-1-85345-255-0

The Divine Blueprint
God's extraordinary power in ordinary lives
ISBN: 978-1-85345-292-5

The Holy Spirit
Understanding and experiencing Him
ISBN: 978-1-85345-254-3

The Image of God
His attributes and character
ISBN: 978-1-85345-228-4

The Kingdom
Studies from Matthew's Gospel
ISBN: 978-1-85345-251-2

The Letter to the Colossians
In Christ alone
ISBN: 978-1-85345-405-9

The Letter to the Romans
Good news for everyone
ISBN: 978-1-85345-250-5

The Lord's Prayer
Praying Jesus' way
ISBN: 978-1-85345-460-8

The Prodigal Son
Amazing grace
ISBN: 978-1-85345-412-7

The Second Coming
Living in the light of Jesus' return
ISBN: 978-1-85345-422-6

The Sermon on the Mount
Life within the new covenant
ISBN: 978-1-85345-370-0

The Tabernacle
Entering into God's presence
ISBN: 978-1-85345-230-7

The Uniqueness of our Faith
What makes Christianity distinctive?
ISBN: 978-1-85345-232-1

£3.99 each (plus p&p)

Price correct at time of printing

Enjoy in-depth Bible study

Each issue of these bimonthly daily Bible-reading notes gives you insightful commentary on a book of the Old and New Testaments with reflections on a Psalm each weekend.

Enjoy contributions from two well-known authors every two months, and over a five-year period you will be taken through the entire Bible.

Only £2.49 each or £13.80 per year subscription, (inc p&p in the UK)

Prices correct at time of print